Clocks We Watch

Mary Copeland

Plain View Press
P. O. 42255
Austin, TX 78704

plainviewpress.net
sb@plainviewpress.net
1-512-441-2452

Copyright Mary Copeland, 2008. All rights reserved.
ISBN: 978-0-911051-57-5
Library of Congress Number: 2008936021

Grateful acknowledgements to the following publications, in which these poems appeared previously, often in earlier versions:

Sulphur River Review: "American Hymn," "Ticking"
The Pacific Review: "Topography," "A Mother Of Invention"
Pearl: "After 15 Years"
Epicenter: "Peaches"
Spillway: "A Virgin In Stone"

Special thanks to Jeff Green.

Cover image by Omae Desu.

Contents

One

The White At the End Of the Tunnel	9
On the Return To Earth	10
The Gravity Of God	12
A Case For Laundry	13
Peaches	15
Topography	16
Weekend At Moonstone Beach	17
Anesthesia	18
The First Time After Surgery	19
A Virgin In Stone	20

Two

Still Life	23
During Math, Mr. Okada Discovers He's Romantic	25
Ovulation	26
Lemon Love	27
A Mother Of Invention	28
The Read Letter	29
John Wayne Brings Reinforcements To the Sick Room	30
The Day We Turned the Clocks Forward	31
Aerodynamics	32
The Architect's Season	33
Gargoyles In Love	35

Three

The Persistence Of Buzzards, Lessons In Patience	39
The Known World: Pulaski, Tennessee 1968	40
August Fireflies	41
Lucky	42
The Movies Were Right	43
Planet Number Nine	44
Recipe	45

Ticking	46
This Is November	47
After Fifteen Years	48
After the Swarm	49
Windowpane	51
The Rats	52
Natural Born Enemies	53
On the Nature Of Predators	55
Divine Errata	56
Having the Right Change	57

Four

Another Route To Heaven	61
Delilah	62
Samson	63
Virgin, On the Rocks	64
Wonder Bra, Religious Painting	66
Spark	67
Bad Poem	68
Brandi, Barefoot	69
At the Getty	70
American Hymn	71
The Effects Of Lightning	72
Advice to Ryan Who Believes Writing Words Like "Boob" and "Pussy" In His Poems Will Get Him Sex	74
First Reader Feminist Studies	75
Ovation	76
The World We Know	77
About the Author	79

For John and Joel

One

The White At the End Of the Tunnel

They'll say it was simply random neurons trailing on the edge
of a synapse, confetti of light scarring the black unconscious—
not my mother, flushed in her pink chenille bathrobe
slurring expletives from behind a door that never quite closes.

I reached toward the grainy blur of outstretched arms,
the path ahead unfolding like cheap wallets
with clear plastic photograph holders,
and a low thrum they'll say was my own heart beating,

not my daughter asking if God wants me back.
I do know I looked both ways before crossing,
was astonished as I felt the approach of her fingertips
tether around my skin as my hands bristled,
and held me here.

On the Return To Earth

> *I grieve that grief has taught me nothing.*
> Ralph Waldo Emerson

I.

Because the hard January rain rose up from the sewer
in swollen pools of mud, leaving blankets of silt in the gutters,

the potholes have flourished like cavities, my father says, and points
to fissures that widen toward gaps the size of a well-fed cat.

Mr. Saunders' teenage daughter parks so close to the curb
the mailbox door won't open

and the supermarket clerk never has learned how to make change.
His urologist had the nerve

to ask if he needed Viagra.
Sleep is transient, heartburn unforgiving.

This is my father's grief.
The anger stage surfacing between denial and acceptance

and splayed like the arc of dust
a child's bike makes when forced to a skidding stop.

I watch him stoop to pull a dandelion from the front planter
and he steps on a trail of ants channeling toward the front porch.

II.

Last week the newspaper ran a story about a middle school kid
who won his regional science fair by discovering

a way to stop ants without killing them. It seems they won't march
across baby powder. I imagine his Hindu parents

taught him that all life is divine,
every heartbeat holy, and when that heart stops,

the soul journeys to some other body.
 He is brave, this boy,

knowing something of this life, his willingness to relive
his days as a spider, dove, sculptor or slave.

Brave, but very young. He hasn't yet held
his dying mother in his arms, listened for the rattling wheeze

to stop, felt her fingers cold as the morning sidewalk
or watched mortuary attendants zip white plastic

across her face. He wins a science trophy and a segment
on the six o'clock news for saving an insect whose lifespan

is, at best, sixty days. Still, he smiles for the camera,
waves as if his arms were fastened on strings spun from some sure
heaven.

The Gravity Of God

That summer in Zion, the slate sky burned to orange
when the sun doused the flat plateaus. We drove the back roads
of Utah, a parade of maps splayed across the backseat
and the radio tuned to the only station we could find, an absurd blend
of modern jazz, new age instrumental and an overzealous disc jockey
who recited from the Book of Mormon each half hour. You had
recently read *The Art of Meditation* and were looking for your center,
which apparently was a place only tribal natives or Ezra, a park ranger,
could find. I had just finished teaching physics to a group of students,
sleepy undergraduates who argued the only true definition for mass
was a priest pressing unsalted wafers on the tongues of the righteous.

We hiked trails in canyons forged by eons and tributaries,
a thousand ancient stories scored in the steep spine of the walls,
and the scarlet clay dusted our boots the color of a freshly scraped knee.
Our third night sleeping beneath the stars' sly light, you told me
you finally understood God and the quantum laws of universal motion:
That the sun, seeming to race toward the earth's rim each evening,
that the sun, sinking as quickly as a small boy's newspaper boat,
was actually held by the fingertips of angels, and never moved an inch.

A Case For Laundry

You know this: Panties are stacked in the nightstand
drawer—the stringed thongs, the lacy black ones
designed to dissolve the blue funk of routine,
the compulsory white waist-highs your mother required
for rare misadventures and doctor visits. And here,
in the cedar-lined dresser, your sweaters organized
from pale ecru to kohl, and jeans bundled stiff
as an unopened envelope.

Perhaps he'd just showered, droplets of water
dotting his arms, the towel banded at his waist
when he noticed the hamper full. And it dropped,
that towel, as he bent to lift, sort and carry your clothes
to the washer, pulling the still warm laundry
from the dryer, the fine fabric tandem with his skin.

He didn't shave or dress, but simply stood over the bed,
folding, organizing, thick fingers fumbling
with the satin strings of your camisole, his hands pressing
your cotton tees, the way a child will smooth
out wet sand. He made neat, ordered piles;
so unlike him to be this deliberate,
this careful of insignificant things.

And you know this: Suddenly you are wet,
thinking about the time he spent
touching the material that touches
your nipples, your belly, your pubic hair,
his sober consideration for all things soft.

So fierce, this desire, to lead his hardness into you,
quick and crude, from behind,

his rough hands kneading your hips;
the force of the thrust as surprising
as the clothes you found, as beautiful
as a florist knocking at the door,
his arms full of roses.

Peaches

Sweet September peaches
from the roadside fruit stand
drip nectar from the corners
of my mouth
their sticky glaze
clinging to my hands

fingers to mouth
I lick
one, two, three
four, five
then reach for another
the soft fuzz
tickling my lips
as I swallow
summer's concession
to fall.

Topography

Tonight, in the carbon winter sky, constellations appear,
a sudden string of lights that my daughter names
from memory. It is cold, and the first winds of December
settle quickly through our too-thin coats

as we stand beneath stars pinned to the patterned sky.
We've done this a thousand times, unwrapping words like
Cassiopeia and *Pegasus* as if they were the most wished for presents
a child dreamed of in the long months before Christmas,

much the way I unwrapped you last night as you slept,
sliding the warm blue blanket from your skin,
while the frosted air from the window panes slid
across our bed in a layer of silent prayer.

I needed to see what I already knew, what I could count on:
The crescent scar on your calf, three faded inches
reminding you to never cast a fishing line
while trying to teach our son about hooks and sinkers,

the slight indentation on the left side of your knee,
victim of the rusted nail in our daughter's tree house,
or the rose-colored birthmark on your shoulder, the shape
of the flowering hibiscus we planted last summer.

Here, on your chest, the faded incision, extending
from heart to navel; and my memory is unable to release
the image of you sanding the new bookcases, then the sickening
paling of your skin as your body folded like an old love letter.

I've learned to chart your back, a favored map
where I recount the freckles spaced like an abstract painting.
The designs I've named: Potter's wheel, piano bench, porcelain cup,
unchanged, anchored to your skin, more permanent than time.

Weekend At Moonstone Beach

Here, where the shoreline tapers like a favorite lipstick,
the black rocks still amaze us, knotted wreaths
of ancient lava poised at the wide mouth of the sea,
bordering the familiar path we walk each morning.

There is nothing new here, no unexpected
treasure beneath the sand,
no place on your body I haven't touched,
no line on your face I have overlooked,
in moon or sun's light. I have no skin
your tongue has not anointed.

So after you left our bed, I thought
how surprised you might be to learn
I was thinking of a girl I'd read about,
found locked in a closet. Separated
as a child from this world of sound,
she could speak no language,
covered her ears when she heard
a baby cry or piano music. Even
after years of struggle, nothing
brought meaning to her speech,
not her longing for food, the need
to be held in the dark.

So I think of her now, how my own language
stutters and fails, how after years together
the words rush to my lips in torrents
then stop for the meaning they lack.
I can not find them, though I try,
even in this light, even as you touch me now.

Anesthesia

Waking, there is brief watercolor light, a muted
    membrane crossing the world, then nurses trailing like ants

from my bed to their station, bringing Demerol and gauze.
    Still numb from drugs in my spine, I had asked for you,

but wanted my mother, the foreign language of narcotics
    warping my words into dehydrated rasps.

Were she here, instead of three months in her grave,
    she would square up the doctor, look over

my chart, demand extra Vicodin, while rifling her pocketbook
    for twice-used Kleenex and half-sticks of Doublemint gum.

Someone in a blue mask says I can go home tomorrow,
    if I can eliminate bodily fluids and walk on my own.

It is not that you aren't enough, standing beside me,
    pleats of worry creased around your eyes,

saying, *they got it all.* It's just that if she were here,
    my sheets would be pushed taut beneath the mattress,

and pale blue slippers on my feet, spacious cotton underwear
    in my overnight bag, along with an emery board and hand lotion;

where, even in this bottomless stupor, the world
    would be certain, fine and clear.

The First Time After Surgery

I imagined I could hide it
beneath my hand or the lightweight
cotton sheets, certain you'd be repulsed
by the mottled ridge
scored into my skin
like the equator etched on a globe.

Until that night, I'd come to bed
only in my mother's pajamas,
as if something she once wore
might make whole again
the defective ovary the doctors removed
in less than an hour.

Before she died, I pruned her roses.
She in her wheelchair, severed stems
lifeless in her lap, explained
about hybrids—how the pigments
fold into kaleidoscopes
but sacrifice their pungent scent
for vibrant blends of marbled hues.

I had wanted you to look
and not look. To trace the scar, still numb
and purpled in the wake of its healing,
with your finger, lips or tongue;
pay tribute to the space that surrendered
the possibility of new generations
for this fragile, transient body.

A Virgin In Stone

> *These are the facts, but the facts are not the truth.*
> B.H. Fairchild, "The Art of the Lathe"

Few stars still clutter the sky
    here in the desert,
at five a.m., before the sun
    rises and bleeds
the asphalt to a slender black
    stream, rising slowly
into the foothills of the San Jacinto.

Here is where they came,
    throngs of the devout
to witness the miraculous
    water-stained image of Mary,
gray and shrouded beneath the last
    overpass hinged to the edge
of the city. But inside a rift of fog,

standing on the highway's shoulder,
    is where I saw a man,
high beams reaching
    toward his outstretched arm,
the way a child aches to be lifted
    to his mother. Bearded hitchhiker.
Divine messenger in a striped robe.

And the people still come
    to search for the virgin in stone,
even after the likeness dulled
    when spring rains faded
to a drizzle. Looking for hope
    in the absence of hope,
the beauty of things we cannot keep.

Two

Still Life

Unraveling, again, the tangle that is my closet
    I hear piano notes thread through the house,
subdued by distance.

It is my daughter at the keys,
    her fine, metrical cadence
        lifting with an architect's precision
to build song from scattered notes.

I resist temptation
    to walk to where she plays,
        preferring instead the belief,
        in this moment,
that real beauty is in the unseen.

My feet pick up the rhythm, hands suddenly deft
    and quick to industry without effort.

In an instant the tune changes,
    no longer restrained by sheet music:
        ferocious, insistent, and untroubled
by a dictated scale or octaves.

My son has taken, probably demanded,
    his turn. He plays by ear
        something he's heard recently,
            improvising a familiar song
that is just beyond naming.

This is no trick: a mother's simple knowing
    which child plays and which waits
        a turn. Even in the womb
they spoke a different language.

I sit on my bed, inspecting the still life
    hanging by the mirror.
        The artist left the fruit mostly   outside
            the bowl: sandpaper skin lemons,
haphazard half-moons of bananas striped in shadow.

What is the point? To keep the world fixed,
    as if memory weren't enough?

 Could I preserve this unbearable moment,
    I'd paint an abstract, like Pollock.

I'd weave my children's bodies, their voices,
    into a canvas erupting
        into an anarchy of summer tomato red,
            beetle-wing green,

and not the sun's smoke-yellow rays,
    but the brilliant yellow of buttercups,

just the opposite of these inanimate bananas,
    waiting atop the wood-stained table,
as if memory were not to be trusted.

During Math, Mr. Okada Discovers He's Romantic

Will she notice his lecture, how his voice resonates
with the same fullness as Sinatra singing, *I Did it My Way?*

He wishes she might raise her hand, ask some delicate
question about exponential function or inverse
properties. She would come to understand
the potential of universal language as he does,
finding symmetry in even the unknown factor.

How she would love his garden, with blooms
the color of dawn before rain, or the hybrid
roses he engineered himself, a blush of bronze
fused with cayenne. Would she be astonished
to see how he grieves for the spider's web
each time he pulls it down from the bed
of Persian Violets? He might quote Byron
before telling her stories of his childhood –
trips to Tokyo each summer, swimming
the tributaries of the *Ishikari,* and legends
of his ancestors, honored Samurai
knights near the Shimosa provinces.

Across the chalkboard, he writes,
What is the greatest common factor?
then calculates how best to intervene
between the classroom's thick air
and the slow incline of her mouth.
He multiplies the problem, divides
by the obstacles, subtracts the remainder.
The sum suggests that tonight, he'll play
a *Sonata Quasi Una Fantasia* on the upright,
filling the air with effortless music,
long after she has fallen asleep,
in a bedroom far, far across town.

Ovulation

Again you're descending like cherry blossoms in early March
scarcely noticed until a world of silent pink
cloaks the grass, weaving a cycle constant as the moon's
perfect shift from crescent to full.

Here is the place you compass toward,
fastened to the edge of a light-as-silk moment,
each hour dissolving with the slow anticipation
of a stranded guest who might find refuge here.

You welcome this interlude: time to reconcile,
though the inevitable *tick* and *tick* and *tick*
hush your swollen resolve to linger
and discover each possibility or dismiss the doubtful.

But this time, even as you wait, the rhythmic beats
lift you beyond probabilities and uncertainties,
and the morning becomes more than just a wish
whispered onto the flame of a child's birthday candle.

Lemon Love

All winter we abandoned lemons for pomegranates,
our newest passion, seedy aphrodisiac that stained our lips
red, an occasion for artistry during endless cold nights
and fifteen years of routine.

But it was the lemons, left untended on the window's
white sill, that paled from green to hues of saffron,
then yellow, in the glare of December's uncommon warmth,
kept only to baptize my holiday pies with their tart liquid.

It was spring before we finally gave up on the pomegranates;
we found the stains indelible, the seeds messy and too slippery to hold.
We remembered the faithful lemons, and returned
to their natural preservative that conceals even the darkest bruises
during brief detours and reckless banquets of seasonal fruit.

A Mother Of Invention

When the goldfish floats to the top of the bowl,
a silver-orange lily pad with wide black eyes
as vacant as your first apartment,
you explain to your daughter about goldfish heaven,
then consign the remains to the toilet
while she prays, *Now I lay me down to sleep.*

When your golden retriever kills the possum
that nests in the wash behind the backyard fence,
you tell your daughter about nature, survival and cycles of life
while you rinse off the blood that stains the patio deck,
as she makes a small cross from sticks
and plants it near the bougainvillea.

After you find the cat in the street,
where some morning-rushed commuter crushed it,
you wrap him in brown paper, tell your daughter he ran away.
You explain why life isn't fair, how endings are often beginnings.
She sleeps with his picture under her pillow,
makes a small shrine of cat toys on her dresser.

When your mother dies, you sit at the edge
of the bed, watch your daughter standing in the doorway,
framed in the fragile light from the open window.
You fold your hands in your lap to stop the shaking.
You begin to speak of loss, but your daughter, recognizing the lie
this time, puts a finger to her lips.
She curls into your lap like last night's crescent moon,
presses her ear beneath your shoulder
listening for the beating heart.

The Read Letter

Scant light stretches from beneath
my son's closed door, scarring the hallway's
shadows with a ragged glow.

He is struggling to read another dense chapter
of Hawthorne, while silence sinks
into the heaped piles of clothes,
though I imagine soon he'll come to the kitchen
asking about Hester Prynne, why she was in prison,
why the townspeople treated her so cruelly.
He can't grasp the language,
words as strange to him as the letter I found
bunched like a forgotten candy wrapper in his jean pocket.
His girlfriend wrote, *I love your hands, your lips,*
as they pour across my body like sweet, holy communion.

I've searched for some difference in his features,
something that might be simmering
like the thick molasses on my grandmother's stove,
but all I see is the sandy-haired boy
in a ragged green t-shirt and patched overalls
who sat for hours in the backyard
muscling small, bright metal cars through mud.

I haven't told his father yet,
keeping his secret in the heart of my belly,
the soft space where I first felt him flutter,
a feeling like fanning the pages of a new novel,
releasing a multitude of secrets
into a world not yet known.

John Wayne Brings Reinforcements To the Sick Room

Because a cough sputters up from my son's raw throat,
I slide my hand onto his chest to feel for the rise of his breath,
as if my simple touch might erase the fever
assaulting his body, adrift beneath a tangle of damp sheets.
At eighteen, he strides that thin boundary between
child and man: the slight fuzz patched across his chin,
shoulders just beginning to broaden toward undefined
arms, a face without the creased complications of love.
Surprised he would ask me to stay while he sleeps,
I watch the shuddering movement of his hands
as they rake at the things he dreams of: the restored
69' Mustang in our neighbor's garage, the *Playboys*
in his sock drawer, the sweet spot on his electric guitar.

He's dozed all night, waking at times to the John Wayne
marathon eclipsing the room with a blue light, that, at times,
flickers across his face in a flash of shadow.
Twitching in dreams, he wakes to laugh, a frail sound
that stops me cold. Perhaps some delirium has collided
with the virus and he is reaching toward a world
from which he'll return changed, no longer the boy
who whirs through doorways, takes the stairs three at a time,
and left once, I'd swear, phosphorous swirls in his wake.

A yellow moon rises, pushing ribbons of amber
through the blinds. The Duke has been shot, in the right shoulder,
a dark stain filtering through his shirt. He staggers toward
a tangled mass of tumbleweeds, single-handedly kills
the roughneck who holds his girl hostage, then heaves her,
crinoline skirt and white petticoat fluttering, to his waiting horse.
It's a long night, John, and the Cavalry is surrounded
just beyond the next rise. You might consider
an extra stop as you head for town. Bring the fresh
young gun you tutored in the art of precision, bring
the newly deputized ranchers, bring the goddamn posse.

The Day We Turned the Clocks Forward

A bloody sunset softens
to a cracked asphalt haze
pinned between trees
and the blank horizon.

His arms are not
outstretched in vain.
She needs him;
she is pedaling too fast,
unbalanced with too much
weight to her left
and her stretched shoelace
is snaking too close to the spokes.
He yells
That's far enough.

The street
is suddenly longer
than it should be.
He stands
at the curb,
breath tighter
than kite string;
her small frame a mirage
fading from his view
in the last shred of light
dusk has to offer.

Aerodynamics

Because my six year-old daughter believes she can fly,
we've moved the coffee table away from the sofa,
and anchored the floor lamps to the baseboards.
We've set her mattress directly on the floor
so it rests only inches from the padded carpet,
and we've taken down the swing set,
removed the trellis leading to the patio roof,
as if we can somehow make the world safe,
fashion for her an egg-carton universe.

Her bruised shins burn in incandescent patches of red,
the same color as her winter pajamas.
Jumping off chairs or leaping from the front curb,
she is so confident in her ability, her arms flail skyward,
as if they might leave her earthbound body
to find its own graceless journey.
When I said the bruises might leave permanent scars,
she told me they were the price of doubt,
so we took her to the pediatrician
thinking we'd either reared a prodigy or psychopath.

Because she wakes early, we've set our alarm
to chime in the pre-dawn calm, and while the coffee
trickles like the crippled bathroom faucet,
we straddle those first silent moments,
calculating how best to thwart an inevitable coup.
I pulled out my old physics textbooks and explained
to her about gravity and laws of natural motion.
My wife drinks lemon grass tea and takes a valium,
but her sleep patterns hover between a coma
and moderate anesthesia, so I doubt
she's felt the light swoosh of wind
traversing across our bed at night, the soft thud
announcing my daughter's arrival in the doorway.

The Architect's Season

> *Everything you can imagine is real.*
> Pablo Picasso

All of the houses on Via Monserate
stand like proud Inca warriors, stretched
in symmetry from the curb's white shoulder
to the base of the foothills. Here, bulldozers
swallow earth, connecting checkerboard patterns
toward the next carbon of terra-cotta roofs
and beige stucco. The street names suggest
that the city planner was once a fan of westerns—
Palomino, Horseshoe—clever enough
for cul-de-sacs with pine fencing
hedging lawns of fresh sod and frail saplings
held together with stakes and ropes,

so unlike Aunt Tomie's house in Eastern Indiana,
a century old, where we spent our summers
climbing massive oaks whose roots fringed the lawn
like a maze of goose bumps. The resident ghost
we named Peter, because he appeared
to be either a monk or priest, brown robed
and bony fingered who stopped clocks
and wrestled with the plumbing at 3 a.m.
His smile, taut with secrets, left us
sleepless, left us with a Ouija Board
and dime store candles and an awe
we thought only reserved for first sex
or magic tricks at birthday parties, and

although we bought this house new, without character,
without a history, from the beginning we noted
an oddness, a presence. Inside the walk-in closet
my skin bristles, the dog refuses to cross
the backdoor threshold. They built this tract

atop native burial ground, I tell our children,
holy men who worshipped the sun and named
the animals God. Look, I say, each morning,
staring into the glare of daylight hinged above
the hills' vague outline, the stars, they are not gone,
only vanished for moments, then occasionally
returned to earth, no longer alive, but real.

Gargoyles In Love

I slept sixteen dreamless hours after washing my palette,
though I'll never use the pure Kolinsky sable again;
the strands are stained in permanent cadmium red,
the precise shade that achieved balance
between a full horizon and the exquisite, cloudless sky.

Notice how the female almost weeps, but not quite,
while the slow incline of her mouth
scored with a dull kitchen knife appears to speak.
She bears a small, delicate navel, rare and beautiful,
and her head tilts slightly toward the north,
so that doves and swallows rest on her shoulders
listening to cathedral bells echo inside the gothic arches.

The male's chin almost touches his chest,
his lips snarled and stubbed fingers clenched in balls
of green-gray stone. From his peripheral vision
he sees her lovely neck and throat, and her thick thighs,
a blasphemy of muscle that dissolve to knees bent almost to her chest.

Their hands will never meet, fingers never lace together.
She will never weave her magnificent thighs around his hips,
or feel him shudder as the hard granite thaws at daybreak,
although their bodily fluids will mingle, but only during heavy rain,
spouts releasing torrents toward the ground
the inescapable puddle spreading,
staining the unbleached canvas in perfect cobalt blue.

Three

The Persistence Of Buzzards, Lessons In Patience

Because the July heat quickened decomposition,
they buried the bodies in shallow graves,
though rain washed away the thin blanket of earth,
leaving heads, fingers and muddied boots
protruding like driftwood in a swollen river.
They burned the horses,
trading odors of decay for burning flesh.

Sixty thousand rotting corpses, singing
their stench on the evening breeze.

Then the buzzards came.

Not indigenous to the area, they swarmed,
mated, and found a home, the guide tells us.
He gestures toward the tall honey locust tree
shading the cannons, the freshly painted fence,
the memorial plaque at the bronzed feet of Robert E. Lee.

One of their roosts, the guide says, and points upward
where branches cradle a nest of twig and thorn,
toward the great black bodies whose heads turn
in unison as we walk past, watching.

The Known World: Pulaski, Tennessee 1968

She had wanted her first ride, and Uncle James, too drunk
to notice the colt gnawing overripe apples at the orchard's far edge,
and cursing *The goddamn niggers marching in Memphis*,
hoisted my sister onto the mare, handed her the reigns,
told her to give a gentle double-heel kick. He spit
a thin stream of tobacco juice the color of piss into the gravel,
as my sister shifted in the stirrups, the horse's slick coat
shuddering beneath the saddle.

The August heat pitched across the farm
in eddies of visible waves, though we stood frozen,
watching, in disbelief, as the mare bolted from the barn
toward her foal. I looked up, to my mother, then father.
Aunt May dropped to her knees, making the sign of the cross,
while cousin Eddie ran for his shotgun shouting
We're gonna have to shoot that fuckin' horse,
and Uncle James chasing her in his flatbed Ford.

When they pulled her from the saddle, my sister's small legs
buckled, and she slumped to the ground in tears,
filaments of brown dust rising like a steam around her thighs
that were already turning black and yellowing
the color of old newspapers left too long in the sun.
Panicked, she had forgotten the reigns, the word *whoa*,
how to stop the world from going haywire.

It was a violent year. Martin Luther King Jr. was already dead
and, as we would learn later, so were the villagers in My Lai.
But at five my known world was small. It understood nothing
of protests, civil rights, war. Only that my mother,
faced flushed and hissing, *dumb, drunk bastard*
slaps my Uncle's cheek, hard, while I drop to my knees
asking God that I, too, might be carried away.

August Fireflies

Leaning against their faded pick-ups,
the boys trace tandem circles in the Alabama
dust with the tips of their silver-toed boots,
chase warm slugs of flat beer with drags
from a Marlboro Red, then stack the empties
in teetering pyramids for target practice.
They squabble over whose fucking Chevy
is fastest, who has the most goddamn mud
caked inside the wheel wells

while their girlfriends sit on the hoods, fingers
tapping to Lynyrd Skynrd. The humid air like syrup,
thick with the scent of ragweed and loblolly pine,
grips and spreads through their skin and clothes,
hormones rising to the fine-tuned hum of summer.
The blonde in the halter top passes her cigarette
around, lipstick circling the edges: little pink smudges
of Southern hospitality.

Without the moon, the only light is the hazy blue
of car stereos pooling across the dry grass like water,
until fireflies silently appear near the fence
that separates the field from the empty highway.
For hours, the kids scatter, chasing the miniature
lights, snaring them in the glass jars, until
a light mist pillows the field, and they realize
there are mothers at home, pacing the gray
linolieum, watching clocks.

They abandon the jars, car tires kicking up a dust
that hangs in the air like a backyard clothesline,
and leave the tiny bugs trapped inside the glass
flashing off, flashing on, under a sluggish summer sky.

Lucky

During my mother's sponge bath, the hospice nurse,
    Marciella, coos in a foreign tongue, then

wipes the ashen awning of her skin,
    slack as an overburdened clothesline.

Nude, she might be mistaken for a Holocaust survivor
    waiting for scraps of food, a blanket, a savior.

We buoy her up on pillows, hoping to slow
    the tidal swell of fluid rising in her lungs,

fog of breath condensing inside her oxygen mask.
    At lunch, I prepare canned pears, cottage cheese,

an enema. Marciella leaves; it's no longer her duty
    to be yoked to the terror of phlegm on sheets,

diaper changes, morphine drips. After another coughing spasm,
    she lifts her mask, says she is not afraid of death. Really.

And just months after my mother is given back to the earth,
    her friend Mona Lee dies one morning after waking

to a pain in her back. Planning her grocery list and a garage sale,
    she gave up one small whimper, then collapsed,

a pencil still in her grip. At Mona's service, her children
    embrace me because I understand their pain.

Her daughter says I am blessed—fortunate to have known
    the measure of those last days—comforting

to prepare, remove dust, settle accounts. How lucky,
    she says, for advance warning, for so much time.

The Movies Were Right

There are sixteen stadium-style theaters at the Riverside
    mulitplex, where I spent my nights, weekends

after my mother died, living other people's lives, griefs.
    I hauled you mostly to dramas: Divorces, affairs,

childhood diseases that left lives fragmented
    in the aftermath of suffering. I told you

I found these burdens easier than my own, liberating to watch
    someone else ache with sorrow. Senseless, I know.

They were merely actors, impersonators, memorizing lines,
    reading on cue, calculating camera angles

to capture a radiant sparkle from the eyes
    to indicate there was hope, after all.

That last visit, I kissed her forehead and said *love you*,
    though she could only smile beneath her oxygen mask.

Yesterday, stepping from the dark into the garish lobby,
    I told you the movies were right:

How, when someone dies, a doctor or compassionate
    onlooker slowly pulls down the still-open lids.

But that is where the similarity ends. Films refuse to show
    how the lids raise back up, due to rigor or reflex,

I suppose, the eyes staring past the now silent
    machines, bedpans, the hustle of hospice workers,

to some indefinable point, fixed and waiting
    in the unblinking light, for the next show to start.

Planet Number Nine

In my recurring dream, she is luminous as refrigerator light
in a midnight kitchen. Sitting on the edge of my bed, a half
shadow that speaks without talking, she moves like liquid
to touch my forehead as if I were five again and tells me:
*Don't forget your Father's birthday, freeze the September corn
for your winter table, it's okay to pack away my things.*
So I begin to believe in the probability of a parallel universe,
that the dead visit from cosmic observatories, leave behind
the scent of Esteé Lauder perfume.

Standing inside her closet, beneath the single pull-chain bulb,
I thumb through hangers, touch fabric that still holds
her shape; polyester slacks, turtlenecks, the black
cocktail dress she said made her feel like Hepburn.
I keep the pullover, her name embroidered in navy script,
and save for my sister the cashmere cardigan.

In her nightstand, souvenirs preserved beneath the soft
cotton of her pajamas. There is a construction paper turkey,
plumage shaped by my brother's long ago small fingers
and a shoebox diorama with spray-painted planets,
the orange and yellow rings of Saturn hinged on toothpicks.

And here, on the dresser, a black and white photo,
my mother waving. The wind off Lake Michigan teases
her skirt above the knees, or maybe it's the way
she leans her hips against the Mercury. She flirts
with the photographer, her face a galaxy of light.

And just months after I've boxed and sealed, and called
Goodwill for a pickup, astronomers announced Pluto
no longer a planet. Even its moon, Charon, couldn't save it.
But four and a half billion miles from earth, Pluto remains
fixed in its orbit, maybe broadcasting signals, faint
communiqués coming, like angels, toward earth.

Recipe

Her script on a 3 by 5 card,
   an archive of ingredients
beneath a refrigerator magnet,
   detail an artichoke pasta
I will never make.

The words are smeared
   from spattered oils—
now an abstract canvas—
   the artist's hands
absent, and mute as dust.

Ticking

Temperatures are falling with the burnt brown leaves;
in quiet unison they drop while night
spindles even closer than the clocks we watch.
Lupus is a strange disease, my mother says.

The trees have casually dismissed their lovers, I think,
staring at the dry, barren limbs;
the front walk's a lonely harbor for each outcast.
The medication has ravaged my stomach, she reminds me.

We will sweep the cellar before the leaves,
set jars of marjoram and blackberry on shelves.
There will be no cobwebs, this year.
Eight years is the life expectancy, you know.

We will crunch the dead leaves into large green bags,
before the heavy rains or snow,
before neighborhood children stake a playground.
It is hereditary, she whispers.

This Is November

Winter, without question, is open for business
and the sky, a seamless shadow of white cloud,
uncorks the cold like a bottle of champagne.
Outside, neighborhood children pause
in the streets, waiting for the first snow.

They amble down past houses, kicking
dead branches into gutters. Already wearing
their mittens and knitted caps, they've replaced
hope with anticipation. It will be today.
Across the street, a calico looks out a bay window.

By supper, the porch is veiled in a layer of ice,
enough to stop spiders from crossing
to the island refuge of dead foliage framing the lawn.
Over the phone, I ask my friend Roe why we sacrifice
the best parts of ourselves for the men we love.

Light frost eases under the door jamb.
Out back, where we might have built the tree house,
the empty arms of the elm twist in a tangled,
lifeless web. Impotent branches.
Sparrows long gone for warmer climates.

Now the neighborhood kids try in vain
to build a snowman. I want to say give it up;
let go of the dirty white ash that refuses to clot,
that will be tomorrow's muddy puddle
casually overlooked on the hectic drive home.

After Fifteen Years

You regard me
like the once-wild animals
we've seen at the zoo:
Old, tired bear
with listless fur
resigned to a life
of mindless curiosity
behind unnecessary bars

not even running
for the raw meat
when they
pitch it to you.

After the Swarm

We have killed the wasps
nesting beneath the eaves
that rolled in
like movie screen credits
in late March after the roses were pruned
and the impatients planted
near the speckled-green hedge
I cannot name.

By mid-April, the first honeycomb
hung above the front door
huddled between spider webs and dust
like one of those tv camera eyes
lurking in department store corners.

From behind the screen I'd watch them;
how silent they were
nesting near the porch light,
circling the welcome wreath,
congregating like gossiping employees
at the water cooler.

At last, we sprayed poison.
Instantly they dropped to porch floor
in little brick-orange splats,
a rusty faucet the children forgot to turn off.
We brushed them into the gutter,
consigning their corpses to tomorrow's street sweeper.

We have killed the wasps
nesting beneath the eaves.
They might have stung company
coming up the walk,

attacked the neighbor kid selling candy,
or cagily slipped through the small gap
in the screen door.

And what if their colony had grown,
threatening our way out,
just now that the roses
were beginning to bloom?

Windowpane

for John

Around the edges of my fingers
grit and dirt compete for the slim space
between nail and skin,
as if they were the same sludge
the doctors must have cleared from your arteries.

I waited all day Tuesday
for the repairman to come fix the broken window,
but finally hammered out the glass myself after dinner
and slept all night in a wide, cool cavern
that left the sheets damp like the soil

I'm standing in now, trying to plant tomatoes.
Pushing my hands beneath the earth,
I wonder what it's like to see nothing,
to be an absence that fades
like landscapes in the rearview mirror,

which perhaps is why I've forgotten everything you knew:
How far to space the vines; full sun or partial;
how to stay warm, when no one is coming
to fix the window in the back bedroom
that welcomes the cold, even in late July.

The Rats

For weeks the sounds were a faint chafing,
    much like distant car tires splaying their wakes
        on the slick street outside. Heavy December

rains had brought them down from the fields,
    their furrows no longer shelter from mud, or sky.
        But soon, they became boxers, furniture movers,

garage mechanics, attic demolition derby drivers,
    rioting along the rafters, their clatter loud enough
        to keep us dreamless. We set traps,

glue and spring, with peanut butter, the exterminator said.
    We plugged holes with steel wool, reset ventilation screens,
        listened for snaps followed by truncated squeaks.

It was the winter our son left home for good,
    our house no longer anchor or asylum.
        Too many rules, he'd said, loading his trunk.

How simple. So unlike our unwelcome company,
    their refusing to leave, just like weeds, their racket now
        the unspoken between us. Nothing worked,

our only duty a prompt bagging for Monday's trash,
    until summer's heat inspired an exodus
        to someplace uncomplicated, more gracious.

They might now be in a field somewhere, burrowed
    where the soil is cool and welcome, foraging for food,
        dirt congealing in fur, waiting again for winter.

Natural Born Enemies

A week after you moved out,
the last of February,
and beside my bed
near the nightstand, a dead sparrow,
whole and perfect
as Audubon might have drawn her
had she been perched
atop the juniper hedges.
Token bounty from our tom
who arrived last winter with a rainstorm,
gray coat matted slate with mud,
white paws stained the color of gutter water.

I carried the bird in my palm,
wings stiff and black eyes frozen open—
as if it wanted one last look
at the world it was leaving—
past the room you'd slept in for nineteen years,
spare now, except for a new treadmill
and boxes marked with your name
in thick black ink.

Audubon gave his life
to the classification of birds,
detailing their bodies and habits
in journals. I too, keep a journal:
silt of memory that catalogs
our arguments over curfews,
car insurance or used condoms
left on the back patio.
And, like Audubon, I thumb back
through the pages daily,

believing the archive of your life
can be ordered
in an attempt to understand
the elementary principles of flight.

On the Nature Of Predators

Walking the meadow's rim, our boots carve a trench through day old
snow until we find a fallen redwood to stand on, our binoculars scanning
the periphery beneath a moon that burns the ice to a sapphire bowl. We
spot her at the edge of a bough, watching until she cruises down in a 45
degree trajectory toward the open field, scouring lowlands for prey: field
mice, rabbit, the sleeping, burrowed squirrel.

The Cherokee call her *uguuk*, owl of wisdom and prophecy.
Her night vision is flawless, her audio perception so acute
to high frequency, she can sense her mark's slightest movement,
even beneath snow. An amalgam of muscle and stealth,
she is a machine of remarkable precision:
fringe-like feathers muffle the sound of rushing air—
the only bird capable of silent flight.

Spying her target, the owl suspends above the snow, then drives
her talons beneath the surface, wrenching up the small, squirming
mouse, quickly cracks its neck before returning to her nest—
where a mother, perhaps, is nursing her restless infant before the strike,
the other children dreaming.

Divine Errata

"All nature, all formations, all creatures exist in and with one another, and they will be resolved again into their own roots."
  The Gospel of Mary of Magdala, unearthed in 1896 in Egypt.

Spring, and soon the daughters of Jerusalem will walk
across burnished sand beneath an indifferent sun,
their prayers as insignificant as the uncounted grains
scrolling toward the Dead Sea's shore.

It matters not I watched his palms unfold
across the dead limbs at Golgatha
or woke the simple minded guards
from their stupor at the tomb's naked throat.

If I write that sin is man's concept, not God's
that the soul returns to inhabit the sparrow's song
then say that demons wrap my truth with lies,
like the Pharisees who speak at the temple gates.

Why seek the living with the dead?
How do you redeem yourself, Peter, for denial,
for doubt? Tell them I was just the woman
who washed his feet, then call me a liar and a whore.

Having the Right Change

You have been away.
That is to say, you have been here, but not *here*
because you found God
on a beach somewhere
near San Simeon or Big Sur –
you can't remember which –
but the where wasn't as important as the who.
You discovered profound peace
and your sense of belonging in this world,
and now that you've returned to the city and Real Life
you feel sad because God's waiting
for you to return to the jagged coastline
of Northern California.

Today, as we drive downtown,
I watch your eyes, sad shadows of gray,
stare blankly at the roadside memorial
of a pedestrian. The radio mentions
another gang-related shooting
just a few blocks away, and a teenage mother
has been arrested for locking her two
year-old in a closet. As we pass
the busy intersection
at Market and Third,
a homeless woman, grocery bag in hand,
walks with a small child.
I hand her two ones,
thinking maybe
God left the majesty of mist-sprinkled
shorelines to exist in this one woman
with blistered palms and greasy-gray hair.
I cannot explain the memorial, nor
the funeral for a two year-old named Angel.

I only know that God's hand,
either salty from ocean spray
or aged like the corners of old photos,
is open,
and I had better pay up.
Pay up or go home.

Four

Another Route To Heaven

Old ladies arrive before dawn, February's fog
a shroud across the concrete drive.
They are garage sale archeologists,
foraging through boxes of clothes
with spotted hands the color of moth wings.
The one whose husband waits in the car
holds up my mother's silk pink kimono
embroidered with tropical birds and beaded
palm tress and asks, *Three dollars?*

A neighbor child thumbs through A *History of Egypt*.
It tells how the ancients dried the corpse
for seventy days with natron salt, then wrapped
the remains in linen soaked with resin, using rags
to fill where skin had sunk to bone.
Not a ritual for this earth, but preparation
so that the body might arrive whole in the afterlife.

(I tried detergents, ones with cheery rainbows
and bright orange boxes with extra bleach—
and fabric softeners, scented with lavender or lilac,
but nothing smelled like her.)

I've been reading a book on grief.
The psychologist warns of a process
called mummification, our need to preserve
the dead; the way we keep a child's bedroom intact,
sleep in someone's t-shirt, listen to their music.

I tell the woman, Ten bucks for the entire box—
everything I'd held onto this past year,
and she waves to her husband to open the trunk,
though I can't see them as they drive away,
the air so dense it is a curtained mantle
falling over the empty street.

Delilah

The first night in my bed your eyes never closed.
Still, the indigo silk you brought
lies draped across my pillows,
the color of winter sleeping on water.

In neighboring valleys
people tremble at your name.
How can a man with bare hands
crush an army of thirty men,
men the size of giants,
brandishing swords cast in bronze?

Near the place called Lehi, they say
God opened up the earth
and you drank from a spring
which gave you this strength.
What did you offer for this gift,
what sacrifice?

After the seventh night, you slept.
The cave of my body ached as you lay next to me.
Your head in my lap, I called upon
my servant to shear off your braids,
and I felt the strength depart your spirit
like the Israelites' flight from Egypt.

Tonight, darkness swallows the city.
Beneath these angry heavens
a storm gathers, wild thunder
pounds the horizon.
They say it was your hair
that proved your weakness,
but it was only your indifference to beauty,
the transience of love,
that finally bled you dry.

Samson

She is winter, even in the gardens
where her maid brings wine, where the moon
turns her skin to blue ice.
Her fingers braid my hair, and she murmurs
into my ears, *tell me, tell me,* while she fills
my mouth with small drops from the juices of grapes,
and I drink her skin, her breasts, as if
I were a thirsting Israelite lost in a barren desert.
God speaks to me.

The prophet Rejah says
the sons of my sons will carve my name in stone,
and small children will whisper my name
when their grandfathers tell of the fall of the Philistines.
Already, I have delivered a thousand bodies,
broken by my bare hand,
staring into the dead eyes of my enemies
while the breath departs from their spirit
in a final hollow wail.

Rejah says I see visions,
that there is greatness in my blood,
like Abraham or even Moses,
but I see nothing past what is before me,
an advancing soldier to kill,
a woman who scents my hair with spice
then lies with me in perfumed linen.

Tonight, the harp player, Celia, plays her instrument
like the captain of a legion of armies,
commanding the strings beneath her fingers
to release their transient refrain throughout these walls.
The threads are willing slaves, her bidding undeniable.
Can you hear it? Listen for each note.
God is speaking.

Virgin, On the Rocks

Inside this restaurant bar, votive candles flicker, punctuated
by the grind of ice in blenders. While imported beer on tap
inaugurates another round of cheers from *Hal* and *Dave,*
their names embroidered on the white oval of their work shirts,
we absent-mindedly watch the playoffs,
raise our glasses when the infielder turns a double play.

You told our cocktail waitress, the tired one with blond
bangs matted to her forehead, *Virgin, on the Rocks,*
so I laughed and said, *Isn't that a da Vinci painting?*
remembering that summer, our hotel
in Montmatre, where the narrow streets
surrendered each night to a fog rising from the *Seine.*
Each afternoon we walked to the *Louvre,*
where we overhead a guide explain

that da Vinci's refusal to paint a halo over
the Madonna's head was an act of hostility
toward the Church, and how the Medici family later
commissioned an apprentice to paint a replica
with the Virgin and angels in radiant
auras of light. He said two versions of the work
rest in separate museums in Europe,
that da Vinci's only true devotion was to the contour
of bone, the cadences of muscle, tendon, artery, blood.

da Vinci would have liked this bar I think—the throng
of ankles, elbows, and eyelids,
thrummed with the music of breath.
He would paint this scene, right here, right now,
would praise the arms of the lovers,
coiled like braided rope, the angular cheekbones
of the women sitting on their barstools, the thick necks
of men chasing tequila shooters with beer,

and he'd single out the brunette, alone in the corner,
where just above her head, the chandelier
reflects across her hair,
like sunlight, like a flame.

Wonder Bra, Religious Painting

Not just the promise of lift,
   but the temporal flesh rising,
as if it were a child's balloon,
   reeling toward clouds
haloed by a glaze of light.

Such symmetry in its design:
   command of angle and color,
union of skin and muscle,
   even the reproduction's
a gossamer canvas like voile.

Charmed, it lures you like
   a noise in the dark, a bargain
for eternal reassurance.
   With a prayer, but no guarantee
you make your purchase

   as if it were armor. At home
you can't help but gape,
   decide even the names are beautiful:
Ascension, Song of Angels,
   The Adoration.

Spark

Steam veils the kitchen window,
while broccoli dips in the double boiler like ocean buoys.
We fill glasses with ice and set the table to the evening news,
considering what motivates a man to murder his wife,
why he cuts her like a butcher trimming fat,
then stuffs her in the garbage with the garden clippings.
As your paring knife juliennes the summer squash,
you tell me a successful murder hinges on an airtight alibi,
while I argue body disposal is the biggest hurdle.
Yet we agree one must manage to appear grief-stricken,
because the spouse is always, after all, the primary suspect.

I mash fresh garlic with a stainless steel press.
If a corpse is buried in the backyard, wouldn't its ghost
hover in your vegetable garden when there's no moon?
It's much better, we decide, to wrap the departed
in a generic garbage bag and take
a midnight drive to the nearest body of water.
Accidents are harder to prove. She might have a slight
mishap on the stairs, been drinking and driving,
or been struck by a sudden, mysterious illness.
I finger the stain running across the hem of my apron.
Don't traces of DNA remain
even when it's been cleaned with bleach?

The broccoli has deepened to a dark emerald,
we heap our plates with antioxidants,
and, determining a toast is in order,
fill the stemware with wine
and drink to bottomless possibilities.

Bad Poem

Dungeness crab, you devil. Skin crimped by sun or salt,
you wait for high tide, then scuttle across the mirrored sand,
your rutted claw trail that trenches then dissipates like a mirage,
your white underbelly a meat I could shred in seconds.
Snared, your fate is the butcher's knife, eyes dim as lackluster
pearls. Less painful, I think, to kill you right now.

Brandi, Barefoot

She lingers on the sidewalk after a morning rain,
her ankle-length black skirt shifts in the breeze.
She wants your eyes on her, the way a small child
will demand, *watch this!* She always returns,

even on the coldest mornings, walking the four blocks
to Frank's Deli, or standing in line at the post office,
while young girls whisper and the man in the navy suit
parts his lips, licking them slightly.

A small pebble presses into her arch, but is ignored.
She coos at Cindy Robinson's baby, pets the stray Siamese
rubbing her calf. She imagines herself Jesus,
approaching Peter and John during the storm.

The women eating lunch at the outside café
wish they had the nerve, emancipated from their
Cobb salads and lemon water. Underneath the table,
one absent-mindedly nudges off her pumps with her toes.

Brandi sits down at a bench, reads from the book
of Proverbs. *She is like the merchant ships.*
Her brown legs are uncrossed, toenails
painted in Glimmering Iced Ruby.

Remember, when she asks you to wash her feet,
the water must be cool and lightly scented with lilac.
If your hair is long, all the better. Wipe it across
her soles, without fear.

At the Getty

Who would have thought the moon,
painted the color of cherries,
could look that real?

It is not this old man, shuffling across the tiled floor,
hands wrapped around the curved top of his cane
as if it were a woman's waist, lingering in front
of each exhibit, mentioning to passersby
how he once studied in Paris.

And it is not that guard, his black shoes echoing
as they clack through the white rooms
while he silently counts the same measured steps
each identical Monday through Friday,
eight to fugitive five, an hour for lunch.

Nor is it these lovers, the man's fingers tracing the tip
of the woman's bare shoulder, her skin
shining like parchment, the fine blond hairs
rising in electromagnetic fields of energy.

And not this small boy, whistling a made up song,
walking so carefully along the lined marble,
heel-toe, heel-toe,
running his fingers along the thick, red rope
that separates art from life.

American Hymn

Summer evenings daddy took us to tent revivals
in small southern towns that smelled constantly
of honeysuckle and musty dirt
and had names that ended in *ette* or *ville*.

Stiff as picket fences we sat beneath giant black canvas
while the preacher pounded our eyes shut and mouths open,
as the hot breath of July collapsed in dampness across
the red-flowered shifts mama had hand-sewn.

Always early, we sat front and middle
while the lost and those seeking the truth meandered
in from the darkness until they found the light—
a hard folding chair and collection plate, amen.

In late August, when the shrieking started,
we should have abandoned our makeshift pews,
to stop the sickening attack of raccoons
on the small litter of kittens

a neighborhood child had brought boxed to give away.
Instead, we sang above the clamor, a chorus of
Peace in the Valley seeping into the aisles
like blood into the gauze of an open wound.

We kept singing. *I'll Fly Away. Blessed Assurance.*
Besides, who could have seen in the dim light outside,
while inside, the blindness raged on, and upward
into the brilliant flood lights of heaven?

The Effects Of Lightning

It took two days
and three sharp blades
for Javier to carve a heart
with the words
Eva will you marry me?
etched on the elm's trunk
like a spider's web.

Pleased,
he showed his friends,
his cousin Rene,
even his aunt Nidia,
who said
*find a good woman
and maybe you will
make something
of yourself.*

On Sunday,
with a crowd waiting
behind the hedges,
he brought Eva
to the park,
stared disbelieving
at the stump,
splinters scattered and sharp
like Eva's sobbing.

It was a sign.
Two years later
he married
his cousin's best friend's
sister, Perla.

Aunt Nidia says
sometimes the gods
make decisions
for you.

Advice to Ryan Who Believes Writing Words Like "Boob" and "Pussy" In His Poems Will Get Him Sex

After Elizabeth Bishop

The art of getting laid isn't hard to master;
Abandoning crude motifs is time so well spent
that your poetry would hardly be called a disaster.

Write something every day. Surrender the crass:
Try reading, no—memorize Frost's, "The Silken Tent."
The art of getting laid isn't hard to master.

Then practice the subtle or sublime, there are vast
resources; Millay, Bishop, even Marlowe's Shepherd went
with decorum, and that was no disaster.

Lose your need to shock, for I sometimes feel harassed,
or defiled, listening to your pornographic torment.
The art of getting laid isn't hard to master.

Write a poem that does not revolve around your penis,
it's the other head we like. Hearing one more lament
of anguished desire will surely spell disaster.

Even pretend sex is unimportant; instead, make use
of what's hiding in between the lines—your talent.
It's evident the art of getting laid isn't hard to master,
though rejection (I'm sure!) often feels like such disaster.

First Reader Feminist Studies

It's hard not to love prudent, practical Jane,
wearing the pink dress, hair ribbons, and lace-
trimmed bobby socks. Unwavering, it's plain
from the beginning she had a plan, embraced
Dick in all his insipid machismo.
"I missed the ball, Dick," she'd say, pointing toward
the picket fence, but meant, *quid pro quo,
you dick, for throwing the ball so hard.
Now get it yourself.* That's right, Jane's not
some trophy, sidelined because she's blonde,
nor the brainless, butterfingered girl we thought
couldn't catch. Take a moment, look beyond
the yard—over there! Jane likes to see her
man face down in the bush. And I concur.

Ovation

For days you've rummaged through antique stores,
hunting lamps, statues, black and white photos—
anything to replenish shelves and vacant corners,
eclipse the blank, but dirt-smudged walls.

You put the ceramic bullfighter on the landing,
how your ex would hate the Cordobon black hat,
its glossed red cape the color of plastic picnic spoons.
A fringe-beaded shade in pale emerald flatters

the floor lamp; at night the diffused glow
reminds you of a massage parlor. You've hung dozens
of pictures: unknown people, nameless, foreign places.
You like this unfamiliarity, imagine a history

for the sad woman sitting at the edge of an unmade
bed. How ironic, that when your lover left, he moved
across the street and now, for the past two nights
you've watched an eighteen year-old scramble

out his door at midnight. You tell the sad woman
you might consider slashing his tires. It's unoriginal,
but less creepy than a voodoo doll. She doesn't look
up, so you presume her non-committal disposition

is an acquiesce. Probably heart-broke herself,
you detect a faint upturn of her lips, though
her eyes say nothing. How coy. You decide
to throw away the mail he didn't bother to forward

and as you leave, the sharpened blade in your hand,
you notice the Jacarandas have finally shed, the earth
layered in purple confetti blooms. Where you walk
wind rustles through empty branches.

It sounds like applause.

The World We Know

Fortunate for the octopus to have no skeleton,
no bones that creak when waking, no labor
to straighten it's crooked back or vertebrae
that surrenders to decay, the atrophy of aging.

It survives, as a body must, by sliding beneath
a slimed jag of coral, propelled by the pulse
of tides and three hearts that pump blood
to eight arms unfolding like an orgasm.

It tastes what it touches; understands
by genetic disposition the merciless, euphoric
nature of survival, so that when the male
injects the female with his sperm, he dies

soon after, becomes buoyant on the water,
like God.

About the Author

Mary Copeland received an MFA from the University of California at Riverside in June of 2007. She currently teaches English at San Bernardino Valley College and is working on a second volume of poetry. She lives in Southern California with her family.

Photo of author by Dana Stamps

www.ingramcontent.com/pod-product-compliance
Lightning Source LLC
Chambersburg PA
CBHW071839290426
44109CB00017B/1869